St. Helena Library

Are you a Spider?

For Tom M.–J. A.

KINGFISHER
a Houghton Mifflin Company imprint
222 Berkeley Street
Boston, Massachusetts 02116
www.houghtonmifflinbooks.com

First published in hardcover in 2000
First published in paperback in 2003

2 4 6 8 10 9 7 5 3 1

(PB) 1TR/1202/TWP/DIG(MA)/170SEM

LIBRARY OF CONGRESS CATALOGING-IN-PUBLICATION DATA
Allen, Judy.
Are you a spider? / by Judy Allen; illustrated by Tudor Humphries.–1st ed.
p. cm.–(Backyard books)
Summary: Introduces the life cycle of a spider, describing how it hatches, develops,
spins webs, and feeds.
1. Spiders–Juvenile literature. [1. Spiders.] I. Humphries, Tudor, ill. II. Title.
III. Backyard books (New York, N.Y.)

QL458.4 A44 2000
595.4'4–dc21 99-045776

Editor: Katie Puckett
Coordinating Editor: Laura Marshall
Series Designer: Jane Tassie

Printed in Singapore

ISBN 0-7534-5243-X (HC)
ISBN 0-7534-5609-5 (PB)

Backyard Books

Are You a Spider?

Judy Allen and Tudor Humphries

KINGFISHER

Are you a spider?
If you are, your mother
looks like this, and
spins webs.

4

Your mother laid eggs
and wrapped them in
a special silk pouch.
You are inside of one of them.

When you break out of your egg,
you will find you have a lot
of brothers and sisters.

You are all small,
but you will all get bigger.

You look perfect.

You have a tiny waist and eight hairy legs.

You have two handy claws for pushing food into your mouth.

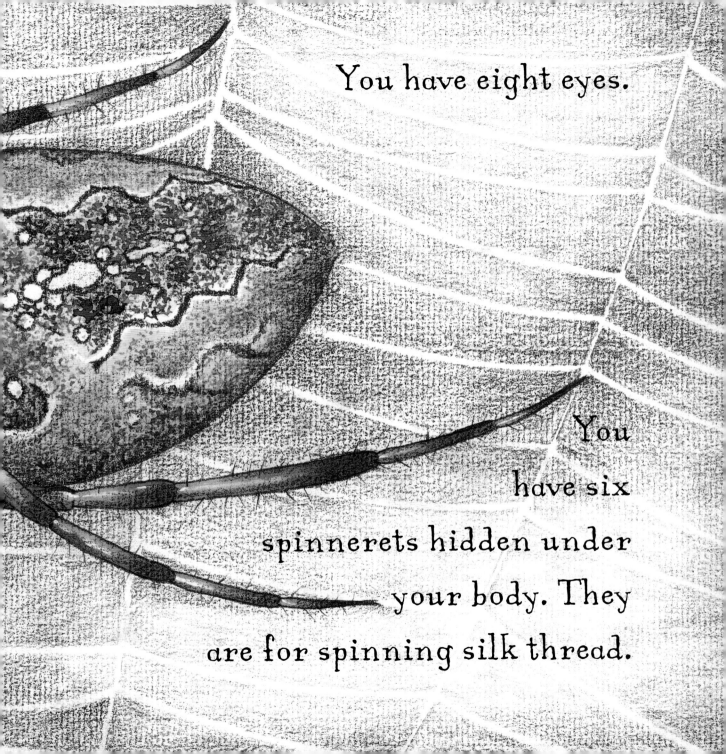

You have eight eyes.

You have six spinnerets hidden under your body. They are for spinning silk thread.

Silk thread is the most important thing in your life.

Begin to spin some at once.

You need it to help you move away and start your new life.

Spin out the thread so it floats
in the air. With luck, a breeze
will catch it and carry
you away.

Or you could just walk.

Use your silk thread as a safety line when you walk.

If you fall, hang from your line until you stop swinging.

Then climb back up it again.

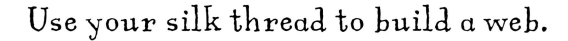

Use your silk thread to build a web.

A web will catch flies,
and flies are good to eat.

Attach these threads first.
These threads must be
very strong.

This is hard work.

Attach these
threads next.

These threads
must be very sticky.

This is even
harder work.

Congratulations!
You have built a beautiful web.

17

When a fly flies
into your web, it will
stick there. Run and bite it.

Your bite will make
it go to sleep.

You can eat it now.

Or you can wrap it in silk
thread and save it for later.

Watch out for birds.
Birds are dangerous.
Birds eat spiders.

Hide under a leaf.
That way the birds
won't see you.

Keep one foot on your web.
If the web shakes, you
will know you have
caught a fly.

21

Watch out for wasps.
Wasps are dangerous.
A wasp sting can
kill a spider.

If you catch a
wasp in your web,
don't try to eat it.
Try to cut it free.

Be sure to keep away from
the end that stings.

23

However, if you look something like this

or this

or this

or this

you are not a spider.

You are . . .

... a human child.

You do not have eight eyes or eight hairy legs.

You might have a tiny waist, but you definitely don't have spinnerets, and you can't spin silk thread.

But you can do a lot of things
that spiders can't do.

You must still be careful of wasps,
but you don't have to bother
making a web.

Best of all, you will never, ever, EVER have to wrap up a fly and eat it.

Did You Know . . .

. . . spider silk is very
strong and elastic, and
spinning it takes a lot of
energy. When a web is damaged,
a spider will often eat it
before making a new one.

. . . there are more than
35,000 different kinds
of spiders in the world.

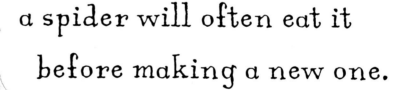

. . . this is a garden spider, but other kinds include jumping spiders, trap-door spiders, water spiders, crab spiders, tarantulas, wandering spiders, spitting spiders, and tropical orb-web spiders, whose webs are more than six feet wide.

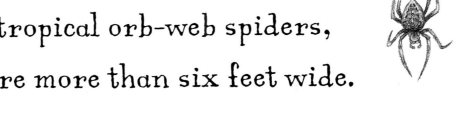

. . . the goliath tarantula has a legspan almost as wide as a dinner plate.

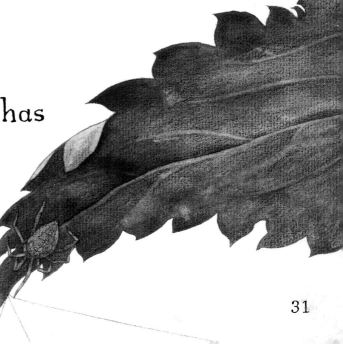